Cute and Creepy Tarot Companion Guide

A companion book for the Cute and Creepy Tarot cards
Created by
Misha Nagelvoort
2018

© 2018 Misha Nagelvoort

All rights reserved.

This book may not be reproduced in whole or in part or in any forms or format without the written permission of the publisher.

Published by The Many Arms of Misha LLC
www.misha-art.com
info@misha-art.com

ISBN 978-0-578-21366-8

Acknowledgments

Thanks to my husband who has supported my art career from the beginning.

To my Dog Pris who sat with me for hours while I designed the deck.

To My parents Mike and Marilyn Lemmen, My sister Missy Somershoe and my brother Michael Lemmen who all have cheered me on as I have worked on this project and many others. And to my friend Kia Bluford who helped edit the text.

A big thank you to all of the people who have collected my art over the years. And to everyone one of my Kickstarter backers, who made the production of the Cute and Creepy Tarot Deck and this guidebook possible.

Thank you all from the bottom of my heart.

Hi! My name is Misha, I am the creator of the Cute and Creepy Tarot Deck. I am also a Professional Tattoo Artist, Fine Artist and Graphic Designer.

I have been obsessed with Monsters since I was a little kid watching Saturday afternoon Black and White horror films. I always saw the monsters as the misunderstood hero of the stories. As I was exposed to other cultures throughout my life, I learned more and more about folktales and Monsters from other parts of the world. Again and again I saw how a seemingly horrible monster could just as easily be misunderstood. Dracula had a blood disease, he needed fresh blood. Maybe if there had been blood banks back in the old days in Transylvania, he wouldn't have needed to bite all those necks. Frankenstein's Monster was just afraid of fire and in his panic to get away, he hurt others. The Yokai Kuchisaki Onna was betrayed and mutilated by her husband, now she seeks affirmation of her beauty. I guess I related to the misunderstood monsters since I was bullied and misunderstood myself.

My Cute and Creepy Tarot deck is made up of the traditional 78 cards: 56 minor Arcana (4 suits of 14 cards each) and 22 major Arcana cards. In researching this project, I looked at many different tarot decks for layout and symbolism inspiration. The meanings in my companion guidebook are based on what "felt right" to me out of all the different decks I researched. Each card has a Monster, Yokai or Creature from Folklore on it. I tried my best to match the story of the creature, to the meaning of the cards. I have a great affinity for the cute, not classically cute per-se, but a cuteness that is there despite the horror of being a Monster. My love of Cute and my love of Creepy inspired this deck.

I started this project back in February of 2014 as a Yokai (Japanese ghosts, monsters and spirits) Tarot deck. I sketched The Fool card and The Magician card but then got overwhelmed by the sheer number of cards and just stopped. In December of 2018 I purchased a new touchscreen computer (Microsoft Surface Pro) and a new drawing program (Clip Studio Paint Pro) and wanted a project that would help me learn the new touch screen and the new program. I couldn't have asked for a better project to work on for this. I learned the feel of the screen and all the fun things Clip Studio can do. But more importantly, I learned about the Tarot.

I figured that the process of creating this deck would take a year or two because I would have to create 78 individual designs, all with very specific meanings. But once I got going I became obsessed with the deck. I spent most of my waking, non-working hours doing this project. Any time I wasn't tattooing or working on the actual deck I was thinking about the deck. It became all consuming and I was able to complete the first draft in only 9 months!

Each card has a Monster, Yokai or Creature from Folklore on it.
Here is the list of Monsters on each card

The Major Arcana

0. The Fool - Dodomeki / Fu Dog	p10
1. The Magician - Jackalope	p11
2. The Empress - Rokurokubi	p12
3. The Emperor - Horned man	p13
4. The High Priestess - Nukekubi	p14
5. The Hierophant - Tesso (rat monk)	p15
6. The Lovers - Frankenstein and Bride	p16
7. The Chariot - BaBa Yaga	p17
8. Strength - Baku	p18
9. The Hermit - Daruma	p19
10. The Wheel of Fortune - Wanyudo	p20

11. Justice - Noppera-bo	p21
12. The Hanged Man - Jorogumo	p22
13. Death - Half Skull	p23
14. Temperance - Karasu Tengu	p24
15. The Devil - The Devil's daughter	p25
16. The Tower - Gargoyle	p26
17. The Star - Harionago	p27
18. The Moon - Werewolf	p28
19. The Sun - Fairies	p29
20. Judgment - Sphinx	p30
21. The World - Pheonix, Ouroboros	p31

The Minor Arcana ~ Wands

Ace of Wands - Ghostly Hand	p33
Two of Wands - Succubus	p34
Three of Wands - Hungry eyes	p35
Four of Wands - Kitsune/ Foxfire	p36
Five of Wands - 3 headed girl	p37
Six of Wands - Garden Gnome	p38
Seven of Wands - Yeti	p39
Eight of Wands - Dragon	p40
Nine of Wands - Zombie	p41
Ten of Wands - Witch	p42
Page of Wands - Firebird	p43
Maid of Wands - Cyclops	p44
Queen of Wands - Nekomata	p45
King of Wands - Oni	p46

The Minor Arcana ~ Cups

Ace of Cups - Ghostly Hand	p47
Two of Cups - Mummy couple	p48
Three of Cups - Sirens	p49
Four of Cups - Jenny Greenteeth	p50
Five of Cups - Hydra	p51
Six of Cups - Loch Ness monster	p52
Seven of Cups - Sea monster	p53
Eight of Cups - Sea Witch	p54
Nine of Cups - Girl with prehensile hair	p55
Ten of Cups - Sea Monkey family	p56
Page of Cups – Water Nixie	p57
Knight of Cups – Melusine	p58
Queen of Cups - Kappa girl	p59
King of Cups - Creature from the Black Lagoon	p60

The Minor Arcana ~ Swords

Ace of Swords - Ghostly Hand	p61
Two of Swords - Futakuchi Onna	p62
Three of Swords - Hungry heart	p63
Four of Swords - Tenome (hand eyes)	p64
Five of Swords - Bogeyman	p65
Six of Swords - Deer dragon	p66
Seven of Swords - Nure Onna	p67
Eight of Swords - Banshee	p68
Nine of Swords - Medusa	p69
Ten of Swords - Kuchisake Onna	p70

Page of Swords - Harpy   p71
Maid of Swords - Valkyrie   p72
Queen of Swords - Dragonlady   p73
King of Swords - Djinn   p74

The Minor Arcana ~ Pentacles
Ace of Pentacles - Ghostly Hand   p75
Two of Pentacles - Deer Woman   p76
Three of Pentacles - Cerberus   p77
Four of Pentacles - Yuki Onna   p78
Five of Pentacles - Scorpio girl   p79
Six of Pentacles - Leprechaun   p80
Seven of Pentacles - Shroomy   p81
Eight of Pentacles - Dwarf   p82
Nine of Pentacles - Vampire   p83
Ten of Pentacles - Tanuki   p84
Page of Pentacles - Zashiki Warashi   p85
Maid of Pentacles - Goblin Girl   p86
Queen of Pentacles - Dryad   p87
King of Pentacles - Ent   p88

On the last page of the book (p89) is a simple guide to doing a basic tarot card spread.

Reading the Tarot Deck

As I went thru creating my deck I realized that I have experienced each and everyone of these cards in my life. I feel the Tarot is a map of the human experience. Many people don't pick up the Tarot because they think you need some sort of psychic ability to use one.

Personally I see the tarot as a way to help me see a situation from a different perspective. Think of your eyes as Camera #1, looking straight out and just seeing what is in front of you. The tarot provides you with views from Cameras #2, #3 and so on depending on the spread you're using. I believe the Tarot is a tool to let you see your question from several different perspectives and allows you to make better, more thought out, decisions. For someone with psychic abilities it provides even more information.

The Tarot can be very intimidating for those of us who are not psychically inclined. But I feel the Tarot is a journey. You start as the Wide-Eyed Fool, and progress thru the major Arcana till you reach The World, only to start once again as The Fool. It's a great model of the human experience.

Let's start the Journey thru the Major Arcana.

0. The Fool

Card meaning: Beginnings, innocence, spontaneity, free spirit, taking risks, resisting authority, following your own path.

Reversed meaning: Apathy, foolishness, recklessness, having difficulty trusting instincts, indecision.

Symbols on the card

Sun - enlightenment

White Flowers - purity of intention

Cliff edge - stepping into oblivion

Dog - animal desires nipping at heels

Clouds - the element of Air

Creatures on the card

Dodomeki (Japanese Yokai)

Fu Dog (China)/ShiShi (Japan) as the dog.

I chose Dodomeki as the Fool because I liked the idea of her looking upon the world in wide eyed innocence with her many eyes all open for new experiences. I choose the Fu Dog because I love Fu Dogs and need one in my deck.

1. The Magician

Card meaning: Power, knowledge and creativity. Determination to make things happen. Tapping full potential instead of holding back, especially when needing to transform.

Reverse meaning: Weakness or suppressed energy. The need to use power responsibly. Using power to manipulate or being manipulated.

Symbols on the card

Infinity symbol - infinite potential of the human mind

The suits symbols - pentacle, wand, sword and cup for the tools of the magician.

White lilies - motivation

Red Roses - well thought out concepts

Creature on the card
Jackalope (North American Folklore)

I did my take on the magician's white rabbit coming out of the hat and made her a Jackalope and the Magician.

2. The High Priestess

Card meaning: Stillness, Wisdom, Intuition. A sense of knowing things that can't be explained in normal terms.

Reverse meaning: A change from stillness to action. Defending or seeking out what is rightly yours.

Symbols on the card

Moon - symbol of the High Priestess's understanding of deep emotions

Veil - the veil between the worlds of the known and the unknown.

Pillars - one black, one white, to show balance (yin yang)

Key - key to life's mysteries

Creature on the card
Nukekubi (Japanese Yokai)

I chose Nukekubi as my High Priestess because I felt her head separated from her body as a symbol of The High Priestess's ability to cross between the world of the known and unknown. I dressed her as a Shinto shrine Priestess.

3. The Empress

Card meaning: Passion, sensuality, desire. motherhood, nurturing, abundance, nature. A muse and catalyst for creative energy.

Reverse meaning: Detachment, emotional distance, Thinking something thru, too analytical. Blocked creative energy.

Symbols on the card

Crown of stars - symbolize connection with heavens.

Flowers - symbol of fertility

Trees, River - symbols for nature

Symbol for Venus -feminine nature

Creature on the card
Rokurokubi (Japanese Yokai)

I Chose Rokurokubi as the Empress because she has long been a personal muse for me and a catalyst for many of my Long-Necked girls.

4. The Emperor

Card meaning: Law, Structure, The order of society. the masculine, fatherhood. Setting boundaries and enforcing them.

Reverse meaning: Undermining law and order, finding who pulls the strings. questioning authority.

Symbols on the card

Ankh-the symbol of life and his responsibility

Throne- symbol of him as a ruler

Horns- Male fertility and Strength

Armor, Ares Symbol on Shield - links to Ares the god of war

Creature on the card: A Horned man (various cultures around the world)

I chose the Horned Man because various cultures throughout the world have some sort of horned male deity that is a father figure.

5. The Hierophant

Card meaning: Teachings, Traditional Ideas, spirituality. Conventional, conformity, commitment.

Reverse meaning: Finding our own path, non-conformity, unconventional life and relationships, challenging tradition.

Symbols on the card

Monk - symbol of religious tradition.

Crossed Keys - Logic and insight

Scrolls and books - Symbol of knowledge to be passed down.

Creature on the card
Tesso the Rat Monk
(Japanese Yokai)

The Hierophant card is usually a Holy Figure passing knowledge down. Tesso was a monk when he was human. I also have a love for rats in general and have had several as pets, so they had to be in my deck.

6. The Lovers

Card meaning: Relationships and decisions. Falling in love, commitment, choices, partnerships, kindred spirits. Being at a crossroads in your life.

Reverse meaning: Difficulties in relationship, trust issues, imbalance, conflict, disconnection.

Symbols on the card

The Couple - the lovers

The Moon - symbolizes the couple's intuitive nature

Creature on the card
Frankenstein's Monster and the Bride of Frankenstein (book by Mary Shelly)

I have loved Frankenstein's Monster and the Bride of Frankenstein since I was a kid. They were my first thought for the Lovers when I started this deck. They are a good example for this card of the choices we all make in a relationship. Although she was made for him, does she want to be with him?

7. The Chariot

Card meaning: Overcoming obstacles, willpower, drive, a journey, confidence, ambition.

Reverse meaning: Scattered energy, lack of direction, self-doubt

Symbols on the card

Charioteer - using their will to control where and when the chariot will go.

Creature on the card
BaBa Yaga (Slavic folklore)

Baba Yaga with her house on Chicken legs was the most natural Chariot to me. She uses the power of her will to guide her Chariot on a path of her choosing.

8. Strength

Card meaning: Strength of character, gentle persuasion. The taming of wilder instincts. Remaining calm and strong even in a struggle.

Reverse meaning: Feeling of weakness, yielding to your emotions and desires. Lack of control.

Symbols on the card

The Maiden - taming the wild beast.

Creature on the card
Baku (Japanese Yokai)

Traditional Tarot decks have a Maiden with a Lion she has tamed. The Baku (eater of bad dreams) was the perfect replacement for the Lion.

9. The Hermit

Card meaning: Soul-searching, Introspection, Solitude, withdrawn from society, meditation, self-reflection.

Reverse meaning: Misfit, withdrawing from loved ones, exile, sadness, loneliness.

Symbols on the card

Figure - a monk

The Lamp - the guiding light of inner wisdom

Creature on the card

Daruma (Japanese)

A Daruma doll is a hollow, round, Japanese traditional doll modeled after Bodhidharma, the founder of the Zen tradition of Buddhism. I saw a depiction of Daruma (Bodhidharma) in a Japanese painting and it reminded me of the Hermit card.

10. Wheel of Fortune

Card meaning: A major turning point in life, usually positive. How you react to this change will determine its effect on your life.

Reverse meaning: Struggling against changes taking place. This struggle creates conflict internally and externally. Possibly a fresh perspective on life.

Symbols on the card

Wheel - The constant cycles that run thru life.

Storm Clouds - Symbolizing the winds of change.

Creature on the card
Wanyudo (Japanese Yokai)

Wanyudo is usually an old mans face, but I made him a cute girl instead. This is another card that just seemed to look like the traditional Tarot card but with a Yokai twist.

11. Justice

Card meaning: Fairness, justice, cause and effect, balance and equilibrium, responsibility

Reverse meaning: Lack of accountability, unfair treatment, dishonesty, legal flaws, imbalance

Symbols on the card

Scales - scales of justice to weigh right and wrong

Sword - The need to act responsibly

Creature on the card
Noppera-bo (Japanese Yokai)

The Noppera-bo, or Faceless-Ghost, is a Japanese Yokai that looks like a human but has no face. I chose her because justice is blind.

12. The Hanged Man

Card meaning: Patience and surrender to the order of things, accept things as they are happening. Whatever is meant to happen will when the time is right.

Reverse meaning: Rushing events before the right circumstances are in place. Some sacrifice may be needed to attain your wish.

Symbols on the card

Character hanging upside down - Trying to get a different perspective of the situation.

Creature on the card
Jorogumo (Japanese Yokai)

I liked the idea of a spider hanging from its web waiting patiently for what happens next. Jorogumo, a spider Yokai, was perfect for this.

13. Death

Card meaning: Transformation, new life emerging from old. Release from old Patterns. The end of something that has become painful or a burden.

Reverse meaning: Holding on to the past, causing pain and keeping from moving on and growing. Fear of change.

Symbols on the card

Skull - The need to get to the bones of what is really important in our lives.

Butterflies and Pupa - Change and growth through transformation.

Creature on the card
Half Skull Girl (traditional tattoo Design)

The half skull woman is a common design in traditional tattoo art. I used my version of the Half Skull Girl because she herself is in transition.

14. Temperance

Card meaning: Balance, moderation, harmony, health.

Reverse meaning: Disharmony, imbalance, onset of illness, lack of patience.

Symbols on the card

Cups with water - The combining energies for a of union of opposites.

Foot in the water - The subconscious, dreams inspiration, creativity

Foot on the earth - To ground the ideas for practical use. Both feet in balance with each other.

Creature on the card
Karasu-Tengu (Japanese Yokai)

Many of the earlier decks have an Angel for the Temperance card. I decided a Winged Tengu felt right taking the Angel's place.

15. The Devil

Card meaning: Temptation, unhealthy relationships, enslavement, materialism, bondage, fear, feeling trapped

Reverse meaning: Freedom from restraints, breaking from addictions, divorce.

Symbols on the card

The Devil - Temptation

Caged person - The feeling of being trapped by your fears and desires.

Creature on the card
The Devil (Christian mythology)

My version of the Devil is a cute devil girl looking upon the human trapped in a cage of their own making.

16. The Tower

Card meaning: Sudden change, a feeling that the structure and foundation you have built your life on has shattered. Leaving a space for a more stable place for you to rebuild.

Reverse meaning: Same as upright, but less severe, but you may be less likely to learn from it. You may blame others for what happened.

Symbols on the card

Tower - Representing the structure you have built your life on

Lightning bolt - The destructive event that shatters your illusions.

Creature on the card
Gargoyle (European)

As I contemplated the Tower card, I kept going back to the idea of what would happen to the Gargoyles on the Tower when it falls. This poor little Gargoyle is in shock as she watches the lightning hit her home and sees it crumbling below her.

17. The Star

Card meaning: Feeling inspired, inner peace, good health, opportunities, hope and renewal. Rediscovering your dreams.

Reverse meaning: Despair, missed opportunities, disappointments, illness.

Symbols on the card

Pouring water - Free flow of emotions.

Water - The source of life.

Star - The glimmer of hope.

Nudity - Her nakedness symbolizes her ability to be truly herself.

Creature on the card
Harionago or Hook Haired Girl (Japanese Yokai)

For the Star card I really wanted to show her ability to be truly herself, naked, but also wanted to keep my deck PG. I went with the creature Harionago who has very long hair which was perfect for this purpose.

18. The Moon

Card meaning: Look beneath the surface, listen to intuition and feelings. A period of reflection that can lead to the blossoming of ideas.

Reverse meaning: The struggle to ignore feelings, leaving you unsettled. Not following your deep instincts. A need to look beyond appearances. Illusion, deception, hidden fears.

Symbols on the card

The Full Moon reflected - The conscious and the unconscious.

Werewolf - Our instinctive animal nature.

Creature on the card
Werewolf (western folklore)

No creature personifies the Moon card better than the Werewolf. The full moon changes her from Human to Creature. In this state she must listen both her conscious and subconscious so as to not lose herself to her animal nature.

19. The Sun

Card meaning: Growth, enlightenment, joy, material happiness, love, success, vitality.

Reverse meaning: The good things in life exist but not acknowledged, things seems worse than they are.

Symbols on the card

Sun - Bringing light to all

Sunflowers - The Sun's life giving energy to plants and flowers.

Children (fairies) playing- Playful joy and freedom.

Creature on the card
Fairies (European folklore)

Fairies were perfect for the joy I wanted to depict in this card. The fact that the fairies are myself and a dear friend (who's favorite flower is the sunflower) makes this a bit more of a personal card for me.

20. Judgment

Card meaning: Decision making, transition, renewal, redemption, awakening, liberation from an old outworn view of life.

Reverse meaning: Stagnation, self-doubt, poor logic, poor or hasty judgment, a change in life is necessary.

Symbols on the card

The Sphinx - Judges who is worthy to enter temple.

Creature on the card
Sphinx (Greek and Egyptian mythology)

The Sphinx is a Judge in Mythology, using riddles to see who is worthy. So she is perfect for the Judgment card.

21. The World

Card meaning: Ending of a project or journey, a pause in life before the next big cycle beginning again with the Fool.

Reverse meaning: Lack of success, stagnation. Events slowing down.

Symbols on the card

Ouroboros - Eats its own tail to sustain its life, in an eternal cycle of renewal.

Phoenix - The end of one cycle and the beginning of another.

Earth, Air, Fire Water - The four elements that make up our world.

Creature on the card
Pheonix (Greek Mythology)

Ouroboros (Greek and Egyptian Mythology)

The World card is the end of one thing and the beginning of another. The Pheonix and the Ouroboros are both perfect creatures for the meaning of this card.

The Minor Arcana

The minor Arcana are composed of 4 suits Wands, Cups, Swords and Pentacles. Each of these correspond to different aspects of our lives.

Wands: Imagination, creativity, motivation and passion.

Cups: Feelings, emotions, relationships.

Swords: Thoughts, ideas, attitudes and actions.

Pentacles : Finances, work and material possessions.

Each suit is also represents a different element.
Wands - Fire
Cups - Water
Swords - Air
Pentacles - Earth.

Ace of Wands

Card meaning: New beginnings, opportunities, motivation, creativity. A time of new action, energy, strength and determination.

Reverse meaning: Chaotic energy, difficult to hold onto, needs focus.

Symbols on the card

Hand - Humanity creativity and spirituality.

Wand - Paintbrush creativity, motivation and passion.

Fire - Transformation and change.

Ace - Potential

Vines - Sprouting from wand represents new growth, both creative and spiritual.

Creature on the card
Ghostly Hand

All four Ace cards have a Ghostly Hand holding the main symbol for the suit. I loosely based it on Thing from the Addams Family mixed with Wispy Japanese Spirits.

2 of Wands

Card meaning: Personal power, boldness, originality, grasp new opportunities and explore them.

Reverse meaning: Openness to change, to giving up power. fear of change but knowing its benefits.

Symbols on the card

Wand - Paintbrush creativity, motivation and passion.

Fire - Transformation and change.

Creature on the card
Succubus (Christian Myth)

I choose the Succubus because I see a Succubus as bold and having her own personal power. Here she is boldly painting with fire instead of paint, trying something new and exploring how it works.

3 of Wands

Card meaning: Leadership, foresight, enterprise, expansion, a new job. Preparation that can lead to achievement and success.

Reverse meaning: Delays, obstacles to long-term goals, holding on to past.

Symbols on the card

Wand - Paintbrush creativity, motivation and passion.

Fire - Transformation and change

Creature on the card
Hungry Eyes (a personal creature I designed, inspired by the Corinthian from the Sandman comics).

I did a play on the word 'foresight' in this card by using a woman with teeth in her eyes. I always think of her as hungering, looking for more in her life.

4 of Wands

Card meaning: Celebration, harmony, marriage, home, community, prosperity, putting down roots.

Reverse meaning: Breakdown in communication, transition, lack of community, dysfunctional family.

Symbols on the card

Wand - Paintbrush creativity, motivation and passion.

Fire - Transformation and change

Creature on the car
Kitsune or Fox Spirit and Foxfire (both Japanese Yokai)

The 4 of wands can represent a wedding, it made me think of "Kitsune no Yomeiri" or "The Foxes Wedding", a phenomenon in which it appears as if paper lanterns from a wedding procession are floating through the darkness.

5 of Wands

Card meaning: Disagreement, competition, strife, tension, conflict, arguments.

Reverse meaning: Conflict avoidance, increased focus on goals, respecting differences.

Symbols on the card

Wand - Paintbrush creativity, motivation and passion.

Fire - Transformation and change.

Creature on the card
3 headed girl (Circus Sideshow banners)

I took the multi headed girl idea from old Circus Sideshow Banners and used her to depict the strife that must happen when there are 3 distinct personalities trying to control the same body, sometimes things get broken.

6 of Wands

Card meaning: Public recognition, victory, progress, self-confidence.

Reverse meaning: Egotism, disrepute, lack of confidence, fall from grace.

Symbols on the card

Wand - Paintbrush creativity, motivation and passion.

Fire - Transformation and change.

Creature on the card
Garden Gnome (European folklore)

For this card I have my garden Gnome lifting up a trophy for his artistic accomplishments.

7 of Wands

Card meaning: Challenge, standing up for beliefs, taking the high road, perseverance.

Reverse meaning: Giving up, overwhelmed, indecisiveness, loss of control, anxiety, depression.

Symbols on the card

Wand - Paintbrush creativity, motivation and passion.

Fire - Transformation and change.

Creature on the card
Yeti (Tibetan Myth)

Here the Yeti stands up for his beliefs and takes on the challenge wielding a flaming brush as a weapon.

8 of Wands

Card meaning: Speed, action, air travel, movement, swift change. Being busy, but a good busy.

Reverse meaning: Delays, frustration, holding off, obstacles in your way.

Symbols on the card

Wand - Paintbrush creativity, motivation and passion.

Fire - Transformation and change.

Creature on the card
Dragon (European Myth)

I chose a dragon because of its swift nature as well as its fire breathing that connects it with the wands cards.

9 of Wands

Card meaning: Courage, persistence, resilience, gathering strength, push forward. Weary but not giving up the fight. Allow old wounds to heal.

Reverse meaning: On edge, defensive, hesitant, paranoia, stubborn, not learning from the past, giving up.

Symbols on the card

Wand - Paintbrush creativity, motivation and passion.

Fire - Transformation and change.

Wounded figure - wounded but won't give up the fight.

Creature on the card
Zombie (various myths)

A Zombie is a the perfect creature to represent the wounded, who are battle weary but not giving up. The hanging paintbrushes create a protective barrier behind her.

10 of Wands

Card meaning: Burden, responsibility, hard work, stress, overloaded, burned out, taken for granted.

Reverse meaning: Taking on too much, avoiding responsibility, buckling under the pressure.

Symbols on the card

Wand - Paintbrush creativity, motivation and passion.

Fire - Transformation and change.

Creature on the card
Witch (various cultures)

In some stories, the Witch is the Healer, quite often 'going around the houses' to help those in need, but quite often over burdened with work.

Page of Wands

Card meaning: Enthusiasm, exploration, discovery, free spirit.

Reverse meaning: Setbacks to new ideas, pessimism, lack of direction.

Symbols on the card

Wand - Paintbrush creativity, motivation and passion.

Fire - Transformation and change.

Creature on the card
Firebird (Slavic folklore)

The Firebird was once a woman. She was turned into the bird by a sorcerer who wanted her embroidery skills all to himself. She refused, so he turned her into the Firebird. Her Free spirit inspired me to use her for this card.

Knight of Wands

Card meaning: Energy, passion, lust, action, adventure, impulsiveness.

Reverse meaning: Haste, scattered energy, delays, frustration.

Symbols on the card

Wand - paintbrush creativity, motivation and passion.

Fire - transformation and change

Creature on the card
Cyclops (Greek Myth)

For the Knight of Wands I wanted a creature that was creative and worked with fire. A blacksmith is perfect for this, and what better blacksmith than a Cyclops, they worked with god of Blacksmiths Hephaestus.

Queen of Wands

Card meaning: Exuberance, warmth, vibrancy, determination, compassion.

Reverse meaning: Shrinking violet, aggressive, demanding.

Symbols on the card

Wand - Paintbrush creativity, motivation and passion.

Fire - Transformation and change.

Creature on the card
Nekomata (Japanese Yokai)

A cat is often depicted on the Queen of Wands card sitting by the queen's throne as a symbol of the her intuition and instinct. I thought Nekomata (a cat Yokai) would make a lovely Queen of Wands.

King of Wands

Card meaning: Natural-born leader, vision, entrepreneur, honor.

Reverse meaning: Impulsiveness, haste, ruthless, high expectations.

Symbols on the card

Wand- Paintbrush creativity, motivation and passion.

Fire- Transformation and change.

Creature on the card
Oni (Japanese Yokai)

For the King of Wands, I wanted a strong creature who could also be related to fire. Oni are punishers of damned souls in Hell, they are no stranger to flames.

Ace of Cups

Card meaning: Love, Happiness, Powerful overflowing emotions. Open to receiving and giving love.

Reverse meaning: Strong but troubled emotions, sadness. need to work on relationship.

Symbols on the card

Hearts - Symbolizes emotions.

Cup - Open to receiving and giving love.

Overflowing cup - The abundance of overflowing love.

Wave - Symbol of the element water.

Creature on the card
Ghostly Hand

All four Ace cards have a Ghostly Hand holding the main symbol for the suit. I loosely based it on Thing from the Addams Family mixed with Wispy Japanese Spirits.

2 of Cups

Card meaning: Connection, partnership, attraction, relationships.

Reverse meaning: Break-up, imbalance in a relationship, lack of harmony.

Symbols on the card

Cups - A vessel to hold water

Water - The flow of emotions

Creature on the card
Mummy (Egypt)

The 2 of Cups often has lovers toasting or sharing a drink together to symbolize the sharing of emotions. Here I used the Mummy and his love having a drink in their afterlife on the banks of the Nile.

3 of Cups

Card meaning: Joy, celebration, friendship, creativity, openness.

Reverse meaning: Stifled creativity, disappointment, misunderstanding between friends.

Symbols on the card

Cups - A vessel to hold water

Water - The flow of emotions

Creature on the card
Sirens (Greek)

This card is about Joy and Celebration. It made me think of the Sirens, singing their songs in the waves and attracting the sailors to their doom.

4 of Cups

Card meaning: Regret, apathy, self-centered, depressed, unable to see help when offered. the desire to be self-sufficient blocks the way forward.

Reverse meaning: lack of regret, looking forward, being self-aware, motivation, zest for life.

Symbols on the card

Cups -A vessel to hold water

Water - The flow of emotions

Creature on the card
Jenny Greenteeth

Jenny Greenteeth waits below the water, all alone ready to grab children. When I read the meaning of the 4 of Cups she instantly popped into my head.

5 of Cups

Card meaning: Sadness, loss, grief, regret, inner conflict.

Reverse meaning: Refusal to accept loss holding you back.

Symbols on the card

Cups - A vessel to hold water.

Water - The flow of emotions.

Turbulent water - Roiling emotions.

Spilled cups with one upright - Hope to move on from loss.

Creature on the card
Hydra (Greek Myth)

For this card I used the Hydra from Greek Myth, I thought it would be funny if the Hydra came upon the remnants of a Fraternity (Greek) party on the beach that they regretfully missed, I used red solo cups to symbolize the frat party.

6 of Cups

Card meaning: Reunion, nostalgia, childhood memories, innocence, harmony in a relationship.

Reverse meaning: Stuck in the past, naivety, unrealistic, imbalance in a relationship.

Symbols on the card

Cups - A vessel to hold water.

Water - The flow of emotions.

Creature on the card
Loch Ness Monster (Scotland)

As a kid I was obsessed with the Loch Ness Monster. So what better creature for me to use to represent childhood. I have the Nessie serving tea in a child's tea set having a little tea party.

7 of Cups

Card meaning: Fantasy, illusion, wishful thinking, choices, imagination, spending too much time dreaming instead of doing.

Reverse meaning: being realistic and accessing what needs to be done. Making those dreams a reality.

Symbols on the card

Cups - A vessel to hold water.

Water - The flow of emotions.

Creature on the card   Sea Monster (old maps)

My very own little Sea Monster is imagining herself in a peaceful pond instead of the rough waters of the ocean. Each of the cups offer her another option of what to do.

8 of Cups

Card meaning: Weariness, introspection, moving on, leaving the past behind.

Reverse meaning: Attachment, a reluctance to let go, stagnation.

Symbols on the card

Cups - A vessel to hold water

Water - The flow of emotions.

Creature on the card
Sea Witch (European Myth)

I love tentacles and tentacled creatures. I had to include at least one Sea Witch in the deck. Since she has 8 arms and lives in the sea the 8 of cups was her card.

9 of Cups

Card meaning: Wishes fulfilled, comfort, happiness, satisfaction, contentment, abundance, prosperity, confidence.

Reverse meaning: Greed, dissatisfaction, materialism, negativity, shattered dreams.

Symbols on the card

Cups - A vessel to hold water

Water - The flow of emotions

Creature on the card
Girl with prehensile hair (various myths)

There are many Super Heroes and Villains with prehensile hair, they all inspired this girl. I loved the idea of her having a tea party in her hair. She is content with the abundant tea cups and confident that she can handle them all.

10 of Cups

Card meaning: Harmony, marriage, happiness, reunions, homecomings, family.

Reverse meaning: Misalignment of values, broken home or marriage, dysfunctional relationships, homesick.

Symbols on the card

Cups - A vessel to hold water

Water - The flow of emotions

Creature on the card
Sea Monkeys (novelty toy)

When I was a kid there were ads for Sea Monkeys in the back of comic books. I loved the depictions of the sea monkey family living happily beneath the waves. The 10 of Cups is about happy family relationships embodies my idea of how the Sea Monkey family lives.

Page of Cups

Card meaning: Creative beginnings, synchronicity, emotional, loving, intuitive, intimate.

Reverse meaning: Emotional immaturity, creative block.

Symbols on the card

Cups - A vessel to hold water

Water - The flow of emotions

Creature on the card
Water Nixie (European myth) (Brothers Grimm)

The Water Nixie is a new creature for me. I was looking for more water creatures to use and she was recommend by a friend. She felt just right for the Page of Cups.

Knight of Cups

Card meaning: Romance, charm, sensitivity, imagination.

Reverse meaning: Unrealistic, jealousy, moodiness.

Symbols on the card

Cups - A vessel to hold water

Water - The flow of emotions

Creature on the card
Melusine (European Myth)

Most People see Melusine everyday, she is the double tailed mermaid in the Starbucks logo. I pictured the Knight of Cups as mermaid riding a seahorse, Melusine's double tail makes riding the seahorse possible.

Queen of Cups

Card meaning: Emotional security, calm, intuitive, compassionate, loving.

Reverse meaning: Emotional insecurity, co-dependency, lack of compassion.

Symbols on the card

Cups - A vessel to hold water

Water - The flow of emotions

Queen - Kappa woman a water creature.

Pink Dress - Heart Chakra

Lotus - Spirituality

Creature on the card
Kappa (Japanese Yokai)

Most depictions of Kappa are male. Since I love cute and creepy I have drawn several girl Kappas over the years. I knew she would make a lovely Queen of Cups, sipping tea among the lotus Flowers.

King of Cups

Card meaning: Emotional balance and control, generosity, wisdom, caring.

Reverse meaning: Emotional manipulation, deception, moodiness, volatility.

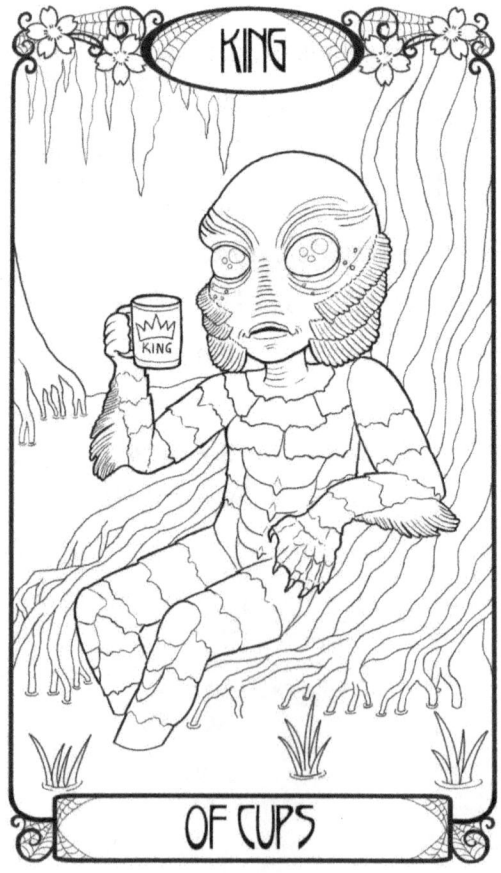

Symbols on the card

Cups - A vessel to hold water

Water - The flow of emotions

Throne on water - A connection with his emotions

Creature - King of the swamp, a water creature

Creature on the card
Creature from the Black Lagoon (American Horror film)

As I designed my deck, I knew who had to be my King of Cups, The Creature from the Black Lagoon. I have always thought of him as Neptune of the Swamp.

Ace of Swords

Card meaning: Courage, clarity of thought, recognize and remove obstacles, think things thru clearly.

Reverse meaning: Fear of conflict, difficulty facing issues, confused thinking. Emotions overrule thinking, goals lose their chance of success.

Symbols on the card

Sword - Silver blade with gold hilt represent the marriage of emotion and intellect.

Clouds - Represent the element of Air.

Creature on the card
Ghostly Hand

All four Ace cards have a Ghostly Hand holding the main symbol for the suit. I loosely based it on Thing from the Addams Family mixed with Wispy Japanese Spirits.

2 of Swords

Card meaning: Indecision, choices, truce, stalemate, blocked emotions, divided loyalty, inability to see the truth.

Reverse meaning: Indecision, confusion, information overload, delays, lies being exposed.

Symbols on the card

Swords - Symbol of intellect and logic.

Clouds - Symbol for element Air.

Creature on the card
Futakuchi Onna

Having 2 mouths to eat with, I often wondered how Futakuchi Onna decided which mouth to eat her favorite treats with. This is a good representation of indecision and divided loyalty.

3 of Swords

Card meaning: Painful separation, sorrow heartbreak, grief, rejection, betrayal, negative relationship.

Reverse meaning: Releasing pain, optimism, forgiveness.

Symbols on the card

Swords - Symbol of intellect and logic.

Clouds - Symbol for element Air.

Creature on the card
Hungry Heart (self made monster)

Years ago I created Hungry Heart with the title of "Try and Touch my Heart". The idea was that she developed an open mouth full of teeth in her chest to protect her heart from harm. The 3 of swords depicts what may have been the heartbreak that caused the open mouth in her chest to form.

4 of Swords

Card meaning: Contemplation, recuperation, passivity, relaxation, rest, regrouping, introspection.

Reverse meaning: Restlessness, burn-out, lack of progress, burn out, lack of self care.

Symbols on the card

Swords - Symbol of intellect and logic.

Clouds - Symbol for element Air.

Creature on the card
Tenome (hand eyes) (Japanese Yokai)

My version of Tenome has her eyes stitched shut on her face and her eyes on her hands open. I see her as being in a semi meditative state, relaxed but still alert.

5 of Swords

Card meaning: Conflict, tension, loss, defeat, betrayal, self sabotage, lack of communication, need to cut losses.

Reverse meaning: Open to change, past resentment, moving on, ending conflict, communication, major sacrifice.

Symbols on the card

Swords - Symbol of intellect and logic

Clouds - Symbol for element Air

Creature on the card
Bogeyman (Various myths)

The Bogeyman under the bed is defeated by the five swords surrounding the bed to protect the sleeper from him. He cuts his losses by taking one of the swords before he leaves.

6 of Swords

Card meaning: Regretful but necessary transition, rite of passage, calm after the storm, overcoming hardship, relief, recovery.

Reverse meaning: Cannot move on, carrying baggage, lack of progress, instability, slow healing.

Symbols on the card

Swords - Symbol of intellect and logic

Clouds - Symbol for element Air

Creature on the card
Deer Dragon (personal creature)

I created the Deer Dragon years ago, I was trying to think up new dragon hybrids. I saw the Deer Dragon as a Calming Dragon, its fuzzy body offering comfort and relief.

7 of Swords

Card meaning: Betrayal, deception, lies, getting away with something, stealth, theft, manipulation.

Reverse meaning: Mental challenges, breaking free, confessions, conscience.

Symbols on the card

Swords - Symbol of intellect and logic

Clouds - Symbol for element Air.

Creature on the card
Nure Onna (Japanese Yokai)

In Japanese folklore Nure Onna deceives a person to get them closer so she can attack them. She herself represents the deception, lies and manipulation. Her stealing the Swords represents the theft aspect of the card.

8 of Swords

Card meaning: Self-imposed restriction, imprisonment, backed into a corner, victimized, helpless, paralyzed by fear.

Reverse meaning: Open to new perspectives, release, freedom, finding solutions, facing fears, healing.

Symbols on the card

Swords - Symbol of intellect and logic

Clouds - Symbol for element Air.

Creature on the card
Banshee (Irish Myth)

A Banshee is a female spirit who heralds the death of a family member, usually by wailing and shrieking. In this card she is helpless, paralyzed with fear unable to stop the coming of death. People think she causes the deaths, but reality she just announces them.

9 of Swords

Card meaning: Depression, nightmares, intense anxiety, despair, worry, guilt. Time to mourn what has been lost, so healing can happen.

Reverse meaning: Hopelessness, severe depression, torment, Overwhelmed by feelings, feeling the victim rather than survivor.

Symbols on the card

Swords - Symbol of intellect and logic

Clouds - Symbol for element Air.

Creature on the card
Medusa (Greek Myth)

Medusa was once a beautiful woman who after being raped by the God Poseidon was further victimized by a the Goddess Athena, who turned her hair to snakes. Feelings of guilt, worry, despair, depression are all normal after what has happened to her.

10 of Swords

Card meaning: Back-stabbed, defeat, crisis, betrayal, endings, loss, severing ties.

Reverse meaning: Recovery, regeneration, fear of ruin, inevitable end, rising above.

Symbols on the card

Swords - Symbol of intellect and logic

Clouds - Symbol for element Air.

Creature on the card

Kuchisake Onna **(slit mouth girl) (Japanese Yokai)**

Kuchisake Onna is one of the creatures whose myth is an exact match for the card she represents. Kuchisake Onna's husband suspected she was cheating on him, he slit her mouth open so no one would ever find her beautiful again. This betrayal, backstabbing and crisis is so much of what 10 of Swords is about.

Page of Swords

Card meaning: Talkative, curious, mentally restless, energetic, rebelling against the status quo, making own rules.

Reverse meaning: All talk and no action, haste, undelivered promises. Rebelling for the sake of it, not because change is needed.

Symbols on the card

Swords - Symbol of intellect and logic

Clouds - Symbol for element Air.

Creature on the card Harpy (Greek Myth)

I picked the Harpy for the Page of Swords because they were Wind Spirits and talkative. They would also steal food and carry evil doers to the depths of Tartarus (Hell). The anarchy symbol on her cropped top symbolizes her rebelling against the status quo.

Knight of Swords

Card meaning: Action-oriented, impatient, impulsive, headstrong. decisive, wildness and adventure.

Reverse meaning: Scattered thought, indecisive, disregard for consequences.

Symbols on the card

Swords - Symbol of intellect and logic

Clouds - Symbol for element Air.

Creature on the card
Valkyrie (Norse Myth)

The Valkyrie were the 'Choosers of the Slain' on the battlefield. They are often depicted flying down on winged horses, choosing which fighters would join Odin in Valhalla. I feel they depicted the Knight of Swords perfectly.

Queen of Swords

Card meaning: Quick thinker, organized, perceptive, independent, experienced, compassionate.

Reverse meaning: Overly-emotional, bitchy, cold-hearted.

Symbols on the card

Swords - Symbol of intellect and logic.

Clouds - Symbol for element Air.

Creature on the card
Dragon Lady (Tattoo design)

I saw my first Dragon Lady in the film "The Golden Child", I saw her again on a piece of tattoo flash (designs on the wall of a tattoo shop) years later. I now see her as the Queen of the Air and this being the suit of air, this had to be her card.

King of Swords

Card meaning: Clear thinking, intellectual, ethical, just authority, truth.

Reverse meaning: Manipulative, tyrannical, abusive, arrogant.

Symbols on the card

Swords - Symbol of intellect and logic

Clouds - Symbol for element Air

Creature on the card
Djinn, Jinn or Genie (pre-Islamic Arabia)

The Djinn comes out of the magic lamp as smoke, I pictured him as the King of Air.

Ace of Pentacles

Card meaning: Security, abundance, wealth, stability, a strong foundation.

Reverse meaning:Difficulties with money, dissatisfaction, fending for ones self.

Symbols on the card

Coin - Represents finances, work and material possessions.

Flowers - Represent the element of Earth. And the abundance of nature.

Creature on the card
Ghostly Hand

All four Ace cards have a Ghostly Hand holding the main symbol for the suit. I loosely based it on Thing from the Addams Family mixed with Wispy Japanese Spirits.

2 of Pentacles

Card meaning: Balance, adaptability, time/money management, prioritization, finding a balance in life, ups and downs.

Reverse meaning: Disorganization, financial disarray, poor decisions, no contingency plan.

Symbols on the card

Coin - Represents finances, work and material possessions.

Plants and Stone - Represent the element of Earth.

Creature on the card
Deer Woman (Native American Folklore)

The Deer Woman worked well with the idea of balance since she appears to be balanced between human and animal forms and nature.

3 of Pentacles

Card meaning: Teamwork, initial fulfillment, collaboration, learning.

Reverse meaning: Lack of teamwork, disregard for skills, no motivation.

Symbols on the card

Coin - Represents finances, work and material possessions.

Stone - Represent the element of Earth.

Creature on the card
Cerberus (Greek Myth)

Cerberus guards the Gates of Hell to keep the dead from leaving. Cerberus usually is shown as a big scary Hell Hound that uses terror to guard the gates of Hell. I went with the idea that no one would want to pass thru the gates, because they would be charmed by the adorable Corgi Cerberus and would be too busy playing frisbee with the Hell Hound, to go thru the gates.

4 of Pentacles

Card meaning: Control, stability, security, structure, greed, hoarding, stinginess.

Reverse meaning: Letting go, generosity, sharing, possible loss of structure.

Symbols on the card

Coin - Represents finances, work and material possessions.

Trees - Represent the element of Earth.

Creature on the card
Yuki-Onna (Japanese Yokai)

Yuki Onna is one of my favorite Yokai, I wasn't sure where she belonged in the deck, but when I got to the 4 of pentacles she just felt like she belonged here, not exactly sure why.

5 of Pentacles

Card meaning: Isolation, insecurity, worry, financial loss, poverty, Hard times, poor health, rejection.

Reverse meaning: Recovery from financial loss, improvement in finances and luck, paying debts, employment.

Symbols on the card

Coin - Represents finances, work and material possessions.

Rocks and Sand - Represent the element of Earth.

Creature on the card
Scorpion Girl (Babylonian myth)

I have drawn my Lady Monsters for two decades now, the Scorpion Girl is one of them. When I was doing research for my deck, I found that there was actually a Scorpion Woman in Babylonian myths.

6 of Pentacles

Card meaning: Generosity, charity, giving, prosperity, sharing wealth.
Reverse meaning: Debt, selfishness, one-sided charity

Symbols on the card

Coin - represents finances, work and material possessions.

Plants - represent the element of Earth.

Creature on the card
Leprechaun (Irish Myth)

What other creature than the Leprechaun could possibly be the 6 of Pentacles? As long as you can find his pot o' gold he will be generous with it.

7 of Pentacles

Card meaning: Vision, perseverance, profit, reward, investment, fruits of your labor, growing.

Reverse meaning: Lack of long-term vision, limited success or reward, delay.

Symbols on the card

Coin - Represents finances, work and material possessions.

Flowers - Represent the element of Earth.

Creature on the card
Shroomy (Personal Creature)

Shroomy is another of my personal charterers that I have been drawing for over 20 years. I have Shroomy and her little Spores (children) standing with the fruits of their labor growing all around them.

8 of Pentacles

Card meaning: Apprenticeship, education, quality, engagement, new job, trade, self employment, attention to detail.

Reverse meaning: Perfectionism, lacking ambition or focus, mediocrity, dead end career.

Symbols on the card

Coin - Represents finances, work and material possessions.

Plants - Represent the element of Earth.

Creature on the card
Dwarf (European myth)

The 8 of Pentacles is special to me because I served an apprenticeship to become a Tattoo Artist. I wanted to do a cute Dwarf girl someplace in the deck. Making her the Blacksmith's Apprentice, seemed a perfect place for her.

Page of Pentacles

Card meaning: Manifestation, financial opportunity, new job, focus and concentration, absorbed in learning.

Reverse meaning: Lack of progress and planning, short-term or lack of focus.

Symbols on the card

Coin - Represents finances, work and material possessions

Flowers - Represent the element of Earth.

Creature on the card
Zashiki Warashi (Japanese Yokai)

Zashiki Warashi are said to bring good fortune, this can be in the form of money, a good job and/or good health. The Page of Pentacles could very well be a Zashiki Warashi.

Knight of Pentacles

Card meaning: Efficiency, routine, cautious, hardworking, through, realistic, practical, a drive to achieve.

Reverse meaning: Laziness, boredom, feeling 'stuck, pessimistic, unadventurous.

Symbols on the card

Coin - Represents finances, work and material possessions

Flowers and Plants - Represent the element of Earth.

Creature on the card
Goblin (European Myth)

I felt a Goblin would make a great Knight of Pentacles, as there are connections between them and the earth as well as with battle.

Queen of Pentacles

Card meaning: Practical, homely, motherly, down-to-earth, security, nurturing and trustworthy.

Reverse meaning: Imbalance in work/ family commitments, loss of connection, self doubt, disconnected.

Symbols on the card

Coin - Represents finances, work and material possessions.

Plants and Mushrooms - Represent the element of Earth.

Creature on the card
Dryad (European Myth)

Dryads are Tree Nymphs and since the Pentacles are about the element of Earth, she seemed like a good fit for the Queen of Pentacles.

King of Pentacles

Card meaning: Security, control, power, discipline, abundance, success, satisfaction and accomplishment, possibly a role model.

Reverse meaning: Authoritative, domineering, controlling, fear of weakness and failure, or misuse of power.

Symbols on the card

Coin - Represents finances, work and material possessions.

Plants and Stone - Represent the element of Earth.

Creature on the card
Ent (Lord of the Rings)

Ent are the Shepherds of the Trees, protecting the forests from Dwarves and other perils. They were the obvious King of Pentacles the suit of Earth.

Tarot Layouts

There are many Tarot spreads in books and online that you can look up, but you can also create your own.

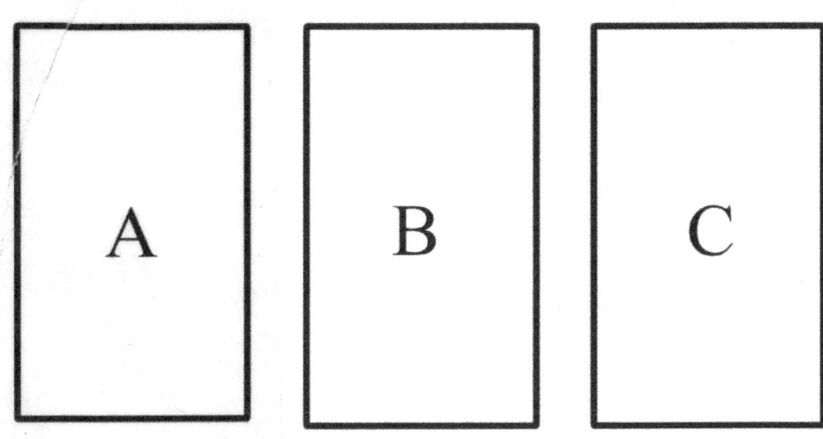

The basic 3 card spread can be used for looking at a situation, for asking questions or for just getting a feel for the cards in general. Here are a few ideas for 3 card spreads:

A. past B. present C. future

A. mind B. body C. spirit

A. where you are now B. where you want to be C. how to get there

A. opportunity B. possible issues C. possible benefits

A. situation B. challenge C. guidance

     Some people like to keep a journal of their readings to look back on, this is very helpful is you are working thru something and want to see how things progress over time.

     When setting up my Kickstarter for this project some one asked if these could be used as playing cards, Yes they can. If you remove the Major Arcana and the Page cards you will be left with all four suits: Wands/Clubs, Cups/Hearts, Swords/Spades and Pentacles/Diamonds. You'll have cards Ace thru Ten and the Knight/Jack, Queen and King.

www.ingramcontent.com/pod-product-compliance
Lightning Source LLC
LaVergne TN
LVHW011429080426
835512LV00005B/337